RUDE HAND GESTURES OF THE WORLD

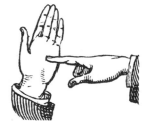  

RUDE HAND GESTURES OF THE WORLD

A GUIDE TO OFFENDING WITHOUT WORDS

by **Romana Lefevre**
photographs by **Daniel Castro**

CHRONICLE BOOKS
SAN FRANCISCO

Copyright © 2011 by Chronicle Books.
Text by Romana Lefevre.

Photographs copyright © 2011 by Daniel Castro.

Library of Congress Cataloging-in-Publication Data available.

ISBN: 978-0-8118-7807-4

Manufactured in the United States of America

Typeset by Suzanne M. LaGasa

10 9 8 7 6 5 4 3

Chronicle Books LLC
680 Second Street
San Francisco, California 94107
www.chroniclebooks.com

TABLE OF CONTENTS

INTRODUCTION

Evolutionary anthropologists tell us that gesture is much older than speech. When early humans had something to say, they said it with their hands. And because manners didn't come along until a great deal later, it seems safe to assume that much of what people said was rude. Perhaps they wanted to disparage Og's performance in the bison hunt or the size of Bog's manhood. We don't know what signs they used, but we can be sure they used some.

By the time history was being recorded, its rude hand gestures were, too. Many of these are still in use today. Ancients insulted one another using many of the same gestures we use now, often with surprising gusto and frequency. In ancient Rome, the gesture popularly known as the Finger was so common that it even had a name: *digitus impudicus*.

Over the next several thousand years, the language of hand gesture continued to evolve, with each region of the world developing its own colorful vocabulary of rude signs. These gestures express not just vulgar sentiments but deep truths about the culture itself. The insults a given culture favors are very revealing. Just as the Eskimos have many words for "snow," so the French have an infinite number of gestures to express ennui; the Lebanese, romantic desires; and the British, an urgent wish that you "piss off."

The language of hand signals continues to grow and change, with new gestures entering the vocabulary all the time. New gesturers enter as well. For most of history, hand gesturing—even the non-vulgar variety—was an almost exclusively male activity. Happily, in much of the world, that is no longer true, as more and more women proudly give the Bird.

Hand gestures point, quite literally, to where we've been and where we're going. They are especially relevant today. The advent of air travel means that one can find oneself in a distant country in a matter of hours and knowing not a single word. We hope this book will make your travels easier—and much more interesting.

It is easy for an innocent abroad to commit an unforgivable faux pas. Learn the gestures that follow, and you will be innocent no more; your missteps will be made with purpose and intent. Let the offending begin!

BUSINESS AND

NEGOTIATIONS

When doing business abroad, it is important to know the local body language. The uninformed can easily commit terrible blunders without even knowing what they've done. Every culture is different, and what is considered polite in one office environment can be deeply offensive in another. In Japan, for instance, one causes affront by presenting a business card using one hand instead of two. Crossing one's legs in Saudi Arabia, especially if this exposes the sole of the shoe, is a grievous insult. Knowing the local customs will ensure you don't accidentally give offense.

At other times, however, giving offense is exactly what the savvy businessperson must do. Perhaps you want to communicate your distrust or to inform your associates they're being stingy. To avoid being taken advantage of, you must let the dishonest know you're on to them. When negotiations get tough, these gestures will help you maintain the upper hand.

FISHY SMELL

Meaning: I find you untrustworthy.
Used in: Southern Italy

In business, it is important to let your associates know you can't be taken advantage of. This gesture informs them you are on to their attempts to deceive. To perform, move your nose side to side with the index and middle finger. The movement suggests that something stinks, and you are trying to rid yourself of the odor.

"I find you untrustworthy."

CRAB HANDS

Meaning: Not to be trusted
Used in: Southern Italy

Although crabs themselves are perfectly honest and straight-forward, it is true that their manner of walking—an unpredictable, side-to-side scamper—suggests otherwise. This hand gesture, another southern Italian accusation of deceit, links the pinky fingers to mimic a crab's movements, implying that the subject is untrustworthy.

"He is not to be trusted."

PAPO FURADO

Meaning: Bullshit
Used in: Brazil

Papo furado is a Brazilian idiom that means "prattle," "trivial chit-chat," or, more frankly, "bullshit." To make the accompanying gesture, place a flat, extended hand under the chin. This gesture, which should be performed only behind the back of the subject, lets the others in the room know that his idle talk should be disregarded.

NOTE: In other parts of the Americas and western Europe, this gesture means "fed up." The chin should be tapped several times to underscore your exasperation.

"That's bullshit."

TACAÑO

Meaning: You're stingy.
Used in: Mexico, South America

Just as the heart is associated with love, so, in many Latin American countries, is the elbow with stinginess. In Mexico the two are so closely linked that a miser is described as *muy codo* (very elbow), the idea being that he rarely straightens it to pay the check. If your *compadre* makes a habit of failing to pick up the check, you may wish to correct his behavior with this sharp gesture. For extra emphasis, bang your elbow on the table.

NOTE: In Austria and Germany the same gesture means "You're an idiot," suggesting that the elbow is where the subject keeps his brain.

"You're stingy."

STICKY FINGERS

Meaning: Thief
Used in: South America

It is an unfortunate fact that, from time to time, we must encounter people who will try to steal what is ours. When this happens in South America, you may bring it to others' attention with this gesture. Simply sweep your arm across the table as if trying to gather any money that might be there. Of course, if you actually gather some money while doing this, your companions will soon be making this gesture in reference to you.

NOTE: In Peru, this gesture more frequently means "money." In other South American countries, it can mean "pay up."

"He's a thief."

GRASS IN HAND

Meaning: You are deluded.
Used in: Israel

As any visitor to Israel knows, the local population is not shy about conveying their feelings openly and honestly. With this gesture, one conveys the feeling that the subject is openly and honestly full of it. The index finger points at the upturned palm of the other hand to imply that "grass will grow on my hand before what you say comes true."

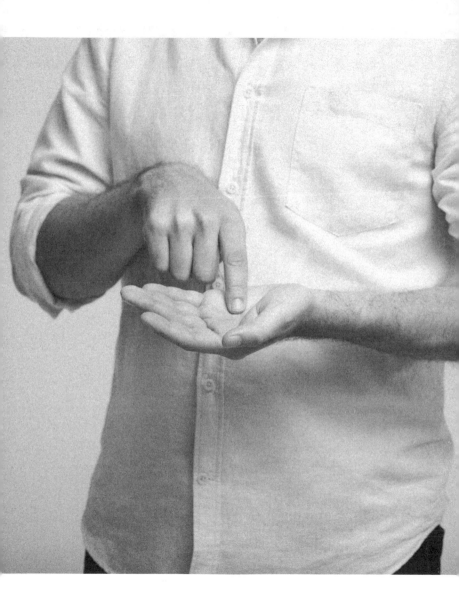

"You are deluded."

ROMANCE AND

INTIMATE RELATIONS

In your travels, a continental sophisticate like yourself is likely to encounter individuals with whom you share a spark—but not a language. How to indicate to the young lady that you would like to get to know her better? How to inform the mysterious stranger that his overtures are welcome? With the international language of gesture.

The hand gestures that follow will allow you to express your affections and are useful even if you are fluent in the local language. Even the smoothest operator can get tongue-tied before a beautiful young thing. Better to indicate your interest with a simple tap or a subtle flick.

Should the subtle gesture go unreciprocated, we also offer some more direct ones. These will not go unnoticed and are only to be used when you are fairly certain that they will be well received, as they may otherwise result in embarrassment, awkwardness, or an aggressive reprimand.

You will note that the great majority of these gestures are native to the Middle East, particularly Lebanon. It is not entirely clear why the Lebanese became the experts in this particular linguistic specialty. Perhaps its Arabian nights inspire ardor; perhaps an admirable native modesty requires that such negotiations take place silently. What is apparent is that the Lebanese dialect of sign language is a particularly romantic one.

RENDEZVOUS FINGERS

Meaning: Romantic rendezvous
Used in: Egypt, North Africa

In many countries, tapping the index fingers together simply means that two individuals are meeting, but in parts of North Africa, it implies they are meeting for a very special purpose: the purpose of physical love. Though often used to comment on the relationships of others, in some regions, especially Egypt, it is viewed as an invitation to intercourse. Use with care, lest you receive an RSVP you weren't expecting.

"That's a romantic rendezvous."

NECK RUB

Meaning: Romantic interest
Used in: Lebanon

Due, perhaps, to its exquisite sensitivity, the neck is considered one of the body's prime locations for romantic maneuvers. In America, "necking" is synonymous with the exchange of kisses. And in Lebanon, a man can indicate his romantic interest in a young lady simply by rubbing the back of his own neck. Those prone to a stiff neck should be careful about tending to it in public, lest their attempt to work out a crick attract too many paramours.

"I feel a romantic interest."

NOSE BRUSH

Meaning: Romantic interest
Used in: Jordan

There are many different ways to invite a young lady to the boudoir. One might send roses, compose a sonnet, or beseech her from her balcony. And all this is charming, this dance of love, but it can be inefficient and slow. Happily, in Jordan, there is a shortcut. Would-be Romeos may signal their interest to potential Juliets by brushing the forefinger across the bridge of the nose. Would an invitation by any other method smell as sweet?

"I desire a romantic exchange."

HIT THAT

Meaning: Shall we have sex?
Used in: Middle East

Should Rendezvous Fingers, the Neck Rub, and the Nose Brush fail, you may want to try this more obvious gesture to invite a young lady to bed. Make a fist with one hand and then repeatedly punch the open palm of the other. The blows should mimic the rhythm of the act of love, like a romantic metronome. If it succeeds, you'll soon be making sweet music together.

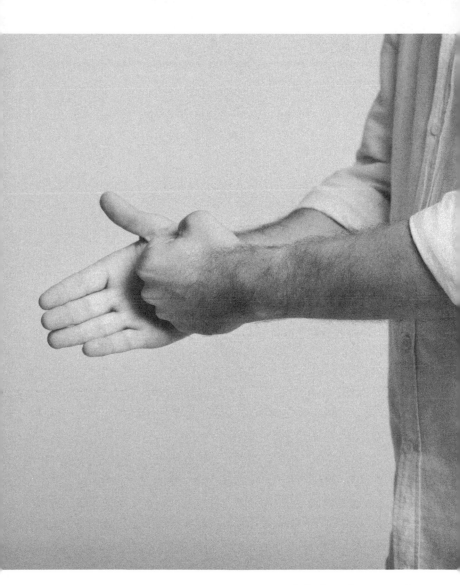

"Shall we have sex?"

31

PALMS

Meaning: Copulation
Used in: Lebanon

In this gesture, the back of the left hand is ground into the palm of the right in a rather artless pantomime of copulation. It is used to describe the sex act but not to initiate it. Vulgar and crude, it serves as a poor invitation to lovemaking, unless the invitee is vulgar and crude as well.

"They are copulating."

HIGH BEAMS

Meaning: I would like to caress her breasts.
Used in: Lebanon and Syria

Yet another Middle Eastern expression of desire, this one indicates that the gesturer would like to caress the bosom of a certain woman. To perform, hold the hand horizontally and rotate as though screwing in a lightbulb. Use with care. When executed inappropriately, it is unlikely you'll be screwing anything at all.

"I would like to caress her breasts."

V ON THE NOSE

Meaning: Sexual intercourse
Used in: Middle East, Central America, South America

In this gesture, the face is a canvas for a tableau about the act of love, in which the fingers represent the lady's parts, and the nose, the gentleman's. Lewd and rude, its use should be confined to locker room talk. The result is an insulting work of art sure to generate controversy and conversation.

"They are engaging in sexual intercourse."

HAND INTERCOURSE

Meaning: Sexual intercourse
Used in: Worldwide

Perhaps the crudest and most obvious of hand gestures, this sign is simple, effective, and highly offensive. With one hand representing the phallus and the other the female flower, the fingers are brought together rhythmically in a gesture that is lost on no one. Low on wit and subtlety but high on clarity, this gesture should be used when blatancy and directness are your goal.

"Let's screw."

BIRD IN HAND

Meaning: Homosexual
Used in: Lebanon, Libya, Saudi Arabia

One of several Middle Eastern gestures that indicate homosexuality, this one is made by pursing the fingers and the thumb together to resemble a pecking bird. The disparaging suggestion is that homosexuals are birdlike in their gestures and that the subject is a bird of that feather.

NOTE: Hand signals tend toward the rude and offensive, and while gay rights have advanced in much of the world, the language of hand gesture remains, unfortunately, rather homophobic. There are many signs for homosexuality, more of them derogatory. These include:

–Making a horizontal OK gesture (Middle East, Mediterranean)

–Holding the hand out flat, palm down, and rotating from side to side (Colombia)

–Circling the nose with the thumb and forefinger (North America)

–Licking the little finger, then smoothing the eyebrow (worldwide)

"He's a homosexual."

SAPPHIC PALM RUB

Meaning: Lesbian
Used in: South America

While there are scores of hand gestures indicating the homo-sexuality of a man, this is one of the very few that indicate the homosexuality of a woman. The gesturer rubs both palms together in such a manner that suggests sexual contact without penetration. Though not always derogatory, it is crude and overly forward. A variant of the gesture repeatedly slaps palms together as if making tortillas (*tortillera*, or tortilla maker, is slang for lesbian in some South and Central American countries, a somewhat disparaging reference to the masculine upper arm strength tortilla makers acquire).

"She's a lesbian."

EVASIVE MANEUVERS

When traveling internationally, you may meet many people you would like to know better—and a few you hope never to see again. If you don't speak the language, it can be difficult to communicate this sentiment politely and even more difficult to communicate it rudely, as you sometimes must. The gestures in this chapter will help you make your wishes clear.

We also include them in part so that you will understand them when they are directed at you, particularly if you are traveling to France, for France is where the overwhelming majority of these gestures originated. This is just as it should be. After all, the French are devoted to the silent art form of mime; no wonder they should have thought up so many wordless gestures that ask you to stop talking and leave them alone. And as with all things French, these gestures are artful and elegant. *Très chic!*

LES BOULES

Meaning: Exasperated
Used in: France

Should you find yourself losing your patience while in France, this gesture will express your frustration clearly and offensively. The literal translation is "to have the balls," and the accompanying gesture mimes the annoying balls one is burdened with. *Quelle dommage!*

"I'm exasperated."

LA RÉPÈTE

Meaning: Displeasure
Used in: France

In this French hand signal, the gesturer cups an ear to feign deafness. This is not a request for you to repeat what you just said even more loudly but to stop speaking altogether. As the French say, "talk is silver, but silence is gold."

"I'm displeased."

LE CAMEMBERT

Meaning: Shut up.
Used in: France

This gesture is as sharp and pungent as a fine French cheese. Also known as the *clapet* or the *ferme-la*, it is often accompanied by an exhortation to *ferme la bouche* ("shut your mouth") and mimics the closing of the mouth. To make the gesture, hold the fingers straight and then clamp them against the thumb, as if grasping a wedge of cheese.

"Shut up."

CHIN FLICK

Meaning: Get lost.

Used in: Belgium, France, Northern Italy, Tunisia

In France, this gesture is known as *la barbe*, or "the beard," the idea being that the gesturer is flashing his masculinity in much the same way that a buck will brandish his horns or a cock his comb. Simply brush the hand under the chin in a forward flicking motion. While not as aggressive as flashing one's actual genitalia, this gesture is legal and remains effective as a mildly insulting brush-off.

NOTE: In Italy, this gesture simply means "No."

"Get lost."

BARBED BRUSH

Meaning: I grow bored.
Used in: France

Another gesture that references *la barbe*—which in French can mean "boring" as well as "the beard"—this one has the gesturer stroke his cheek as if checking for facial hair. The implication is that the subject has been droning on so long that the listener has grown a full beard. To avoid this insult, visitors to France would do well to keep their conversations as short as their stubble.

"I grow bored."

ON SE TIRE

Meaning: Get lost.
Used in: France, Belgium, Greece, Italy, Spain, Tunisia, Yugoslavia

In this gesture of dismissal, the left hand chops or clamps down on the right wrist, forcing the right hand to flick up. The chopping motion mimics the severing of a thief's hand and tells the subject he deserves to be banished like a common bandit. The gesture can also be used without insulting intent to signify "Let's go."

"Get lost."

LA FLUTE

Meaning: I tire of your made-up nonsense.
Used in: France

Yet another French expression of impatience, this one requires the gesturer to play an imaginary flute. He thus connotes his weariness with the dubious story, suggesting that the subject's falsehood become as long-winded as an endless flute solo. Should you be on the receiving end of such a gesture, it is best to switch to another conversational key or silence your instrument altogether.

"I tire of your made-up nonsense."

WRITE-OFF

Meaning: I am ignoring you.
Used in: Greece

The literal translation of *st'arxidia mou*, the phrase that accompanies this gesture, is "I write it on my testicles." And while there may well be people who, out of a strange psychological compulsion or simply boredom, actually write on their testicles, here the threat is simply metaphorical and tells the subject you're ignoring him. One needn't possess testicles to use the gesture, which is employed by men and women alike.

"I am ignoring you."

DIPLOMACY

It is an unfortunate fact that there are stupid, lazy, and ugly people all over the world, and many of them are unaware of their own shortcomings. Ideally one would be able to keep such criticisms to oneself, but circumstances may dictate that you share your feelings. Perhaps you need to let your English student know his work is not up to par, or maybe you must suggest that your neighbor see a mental health professional. Perhaps you must tell your driver that he is lazy or your would-be Internet bride that she is less attractive than you were expecting. Sometimes difficult sentiments must be shared.

Whatever the message, it is important that it be conveyed diplomatically. The gestures in this chapter will let you share bad news, if not with sensitivity, at least with humor. Many may also be used playfully. They all will help you say what you can't say out loud.

ESTÚPIDO

Meaning: You are very stupid.
Used in: South America

It is impolite to point out the stupidity of others, but sometimes it must be done. In parts of South America, it can be accomplished simply and directly by holding out the hand with the palm up and all fingers spread. The gesture is an expression of exasperation with the subject's hopeless incompetence. Even the biggest imbecile is sure to understand this message.

"You are very stupid."

IDIOTA

Meaning: Are you an idiot?
Used in: Brazil

Another South American gesture indicating stupidity, this one requires improv skills and an actorly flair. To perform, put your fist to your forehead while making a comical overbite. The gesture is most effective when accented with multiple grunts of arrr, arrr. When executed correctly, you will be rewarded with appreciative laughs, though not, perhaps, from your subject.

"Are you an idiot?"

STUPID HEAD

Meaning: You are stupid and/or crazy.
Used in: Japan

In Japan, stupidity is indicated by this gesture, in which you point an index finger at your temple and rotate the finger twice. If the subject's stupidity is insufficiently expressed by this maneuver, you may increase the insult by opening the hand abruptly and shouting "Pah!" The gesture can be used both seriously and in jest, so if offense is your intent, be sure to perform it aggressively. If even more aggression is required, consider slapping the subject on the back of the head while yelling *"Baka!"* ("You fool!").

"You are stupid and crazy."

BUSU

Meaning: Ugly
Used in: Japan

If the subject is not just stupid but ugly, you may add insult to injury with this gesture. To execute the maneuver—which is used to comment on the unattractiveness of a woman—push the nose up with the index finger. This mimics the snout of a pig, which the Japanese find especially repulsive, as prominent nostrils are not considered attractive. In Japan, it is also considered somewhat repulsive to blow your nose in public. Should you do so, you may get to witness the Busu gesture for yourself.

"You are ugly."

PEPPER MILL

Meaning: Crazy
Used in: Southern Italy

In southern Italy, craziness is indicated by this gesture, in which one mimics the grinding of a pepper mill. The implication is that the subject's addled brain is whirring as fast as the mill's blades.

"You are crazy."

HUEVON

Meaning: What uncomfortably large testicles you have.
Used in: Latin America, Mexico

The medical term for enlarged testicles is orchitis, and it is a condition requiring medical attention. Here the suggestion is not that the subject may be ill, but that his oversized genitalia are making him lazy and, perhaps, rendering him undesirable to women. To make the gesture, which is used only between men, simply cup a palm upward, as if holding something heavy. Medical attention is not required, but an apology may be.

"What uncomfortably large testicles you have."

QUEEN ANNE'S FAN

Meaning: Mockery
Used in: Worldwide

This very old gesture has a single meaning—mockery—but several dozen monikers. In England alone, it is known by sixteen different names, including "cocking a snook" (that is, making a snout) and Queen Anne's Fan, a reference to the sign language of fans that became popular during Queen Anne's reign in the eighteenth century. Its origins are unknown, but it is surmised that the gesture is meant to mimic a deformed nose or a cock's comb. The insult it delivers is mild and playful. For added whimsy, waggle the fingers or line up the second hand behind the first.

"I mock you."

LEFT HAND

Meaning: I am touching you or your food with the hand I just wiped myself with.
Used in: Islamic countries

While not a rude gesture per se, using one's left hand in any Islamic country is a faux pas sure to cause offense and discomfort. In these regions, the left hand is traditionally reserved for bodily hygiene, and to offer food or a handshake with that hand is to invite revulsion, not to mention fears of hepatitis. Limit use of your left hand unless revulsion is your intent.

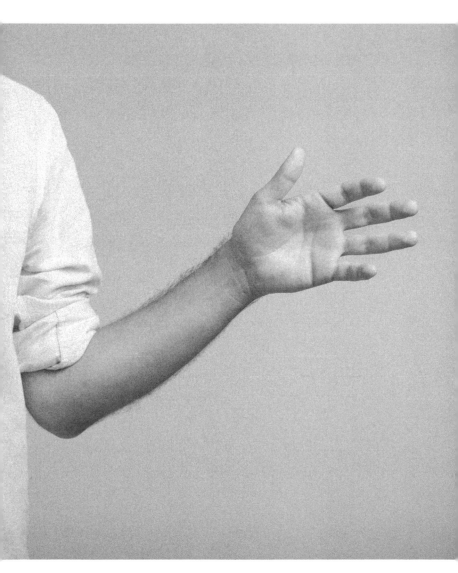

"I am touching you or your food with the hand I just wiped myself with."

ADVANCED DIPLOMACY

Some messages can't be expressed through jokes or subtle hints. When you truly need to give insult, the kid gloves must be removed. Direct and forthright communication is required. The frank gestures in this chapter will express your point clearly, whether that point is that you'd like to rub excrement in the subject's face or that his mother is a prostitute.

Be warned that the gestures that follow are highly inflammatory. Some are illegal, some are ill advised, and all are incredibly offensive. Fisticuffs, destruction of property, and ejection from the premises are virtually guaranteed. Rioting is a distinct possibility. They are to be used only as a measure of last resort.

But as any adventurer knows, a last resort is sometimes necessary. When it's time to get your hands dirty, these filthy hand gestures will do the job.

DONKEY RIDE

Meaning: I will ride you like a donkey.
Used in: Saudi Arabia

An elaborate two-handed gesture, this sign is like a puppet show in which the fingers act out an intricate maneuver whose message is "I will ride you like a donkey." To make the gesture, form an upside-down V (representing the rider's legs) with the first two fingers of your right hand and then straddle the left forefinger (representing the donkey). Orchestrating this gesture does not take much less effort than actually mounting the subject, but it is considerably less awkward.

"I will ride you like a donkey."

FIVE FATHERS

Meaning: You have five fathers, i.e., your mother is a whore.
Used in: Arab countries, Caribbean

If you are looking to get yourself deported from Saudi Arabia—possibly amid a riot—you can do no better than the Five Fathers gesture. The most inflammatory hand gesture in the Arab world, this sign accuses the subject's mother of cavorting with every Tom, Dick, and Mustafa, implying that she had so many suitors that paternity is impossible to determine. To execute, point your left index finger at your right hand, while pursing all fingers of the right hand together. The insult is extreme and almost certain to provoke violence.

"Your mother is a whore."

HERE, DOGGIE

Meaning: Come here, you lowly dog.
Used in: The Philippines

When beckoning a companion in the Philippines, be sure to point the hand down, moving the fingers in a sort of pawing motion. The upturned forefinger beckon is used only for dogs, and to use it on a person implies that you think he is one. This is a highly offensive maneuver and is taken very seriously, sometimes resulting in the gesturer's arrest. A dog may be man's best friend, but should you use it on your human best friend, your best friend he will be no longer.

"Come here, you lowly dog."

MOUTZA

Meaning: To hell with you! / I rub shit in your face! / I'm going to violate your sister! / I'm going to violate your entire family, including your dog!
Used in: Greece, Africa, Pakistan

The Moutza is among the most complex of hand gestures, as elaborate and ancient as a Japanese tea ceremony. Perhaps the oldest offensive hand signal still in use, the Moutza originated in ancient Byzantium, where it was the custom for criminals to be chained to a donkey and displayed on the street. There, local townsfolk might add to their humiliation by rubbing dirt, feces, and ashes (*moutzos* in medieval Greek) into their faces.

Now that the advent of modern sewage systems and antismoking laws means that these materials are no longer readily available, the Moutza is a symbolic stand-in. In Greece, it is often accompanied by commands including *par'ta* ("take these") or *órse* ("there you go"). Over the years, the versatile Moutza has acquired more connotations, including a sexual one, in which the five extended fingers suggest the five sexual acts the gesturer would like to perform with the subject's willing sister.

The Moutza has many variations, each appropriate to its own occasion. See variations on the following pages.

CLASSIC MOUTZA

In the classic or full Moutza, all five fingers are extended at face level with the palm facing out. Appropriate times to use this gesture are when one is disrespected in traffic or when confronting an insolent service person.

"To hell with you!"

DOUBLE MOUTZA

When one wishes to express more ire than the classic Moutza permits, for example, as a prelude to a bar fight, the double Moutza is called for. In this variation, both hands assume the full Moutza position. The palm of one hand is then smacked against the back of the other. Perform this gesture as close as possible to the face of the subject to indicate extreme perturbation.

"I rub shit in your face!"

TRIPLE MOUTZA

If double Moutza does not have the desired effect, the gesturer
may proceed to triple Moutza. Position both hands in full Moutza;
then extend a foot for three times the Moutza insult. Employ only
when discovering one's spouse with one's best friend or on occa-
sions when maximun provocation is desired.

"I'm going to violate your sister!"

VARIATION 4.
QUADRUPLE MOUTZA

To be used only in extreme cases, such as prison riots. The gesturer, who must be seated, extends both hands in full Moutza as well as both feet. The insult is severe and irremediable. Use only with strangers, as no existing relationship will survive such an affront.

"I'm going to violate your entire family, including your dog!"

BEAST

Meaning: You're a beast.
Used in: Japan

This highly insulting gesture is unique to Japan. In execution, it is similar to the Moutza (page 88), but only four fingers are deployed, representing the four legs of an animal. The gesture references the oppressed *eta* (literally, "filthy mass") caste who were associated with four-legged animals due to their employment in slaughter-houses and leather workshops.

"You're a beast."

WANKER

Meaning: Masturbation
Used in: North America, United Kingdom

In this coarse and explicit gesture, the hand is jerked repeatedly in a pantomime of male self-pleasure. The implication is that the subject is so hopeless that masturbation is his only recourse to sexual satisfaction. Its natural habitat is the football arena, where it is often employed by fans against the opposing team.

"Go masturbate."

DICK HEAD

Meaning: You are a dick head.
Used in: United Kingdom

The unicorn is a rare mythical creature. This gesture, in which the forehead sports not a magical horn but an imaginary phallus, is an altogether more common and pedestrian event. To execute, simply bring the fingers and thumb together in a circle as if holding a phallus, and place hand near forehead. Often seen in pubs, at sporting matches, and in traffic altercations, it is used throughout the United Kingdom, where it serves, in the local parlance, to "take the piss" out of the subject.

"You are a dick head."

ARM THRUST

Meaning: Prostitute
Used in: South America

It is in poor taste to comment on a woman's virtue, but if poor taste is your aim, this gesture will suit your purpose quite well. Hold the arm flat across the body with fingers extended and then quickly move the arm back and forth as though mimicking the thrusts of copulation. The resulting gesture suggests that the lady in question is a prostitute and that you yourself are a cad.

"She's a prostitute."

THE CONCHA

Meaning: Your mother has dried-up lady parts
Used in: Chile, Argentina

In most of the world, this gesture simply means "hungry," but in Chile and Argentina, it means something quite different. This rather offensive gesture is short for *concha de tu madre* and refers to the "shell"—or love canal—of the subject's mother. The insult further implies that it is not a well-watered canal at all, but a dry riverbed.

"Your mother has dried-up lady parts."

CORNA

Meaning: Your wife is unfaithful.
Used in: The Baltics, Brazil, Colombia, Italy, Portugal, Spain

Informing a friend that his wife has been unfaithful is an unhappy and delicate task. Fortunately, in many countries, it is simple to do: one simply gives him the Corna. A very old sign, the Corna dates back at least 2,500 years and represents a bull's horns (bulls were commonly castrated to make them calmer).

Be warned that while the gesture is used throughout the world, its meaning varies greatly from country to country. In many countries, it is simply an expression of good luck; in others, it demonstrates an affection for a certain sporting team or musical group. Should you be on the receiving end of the gesture, before you cast out your wife, remember that your pal may simply be saying she is a fan of American college football or heavy metal bands.

NOTE: In Saudi Arabia, Syria, and Lebanon, one makes a similar gesture with an identical meaning by fanning out the fingers and placing the hands by the ears to mimic a stag.

"Your wife is unfaithful."

CUTIS

Meaning: Screw you and your whole family.
Used in: India, Pakistan

Should you find yourself in India or Pakistan, wishing to insult not just your host but your host's entire family, look no further than the Cutis gesture. Its origins are unknown, but its effect is swift and severe. Simply make a fist then flick the thumb off the front teeth while exclaiming *cutta!* ("Screw you!") In short order, you will find yourself ejected from the premises, your mission to offend thoroughly accomplished.

"Screw you!"

FODEU

Meaning: We're screwed. Screw you.
Used in: Brazil, France, Italy, Spain, South America

Fodeu, a vulgar term meaning "screwed," can imply that things are all screwed up or that the subject should go screw himself. To make the gesture, pound the open palm of one hand on top of the fist of the other. The motion should mimic the thrusts of sexual intercourse.

"We're screwed."

ONWARD AND UPWARD

With this chapter we arrive, quite literally, at the end, with a collection of gestures referencing the backside and its orifices. These gestures come from all over the world. For while every culture is different, almost all of them offer a gesture that suggests the subject ram something up his rectum. Some may call for a finger and some a forearm, and they vary with regard to circumference and force. But, ultimately, they all mean the same thing: "Up yours."

And this sentiment is also a very old one. Many of these gestures date back to ancient times, but the sentiment they convey is unchanged. It's a sentiment that's not even limited to our own species; some of these gestures are very similar to ones made by apes.

Although the message may be crude, it is nice to know that the same gesture would be understood by a chimpanzee, an ancient Roman, and a modern teenager. It is a happy reminder that while we may look different and talk differently, at bottom, we're all the same.

BRAS D'HONNEUR

Meaning: Up yours.
Used in: Eastern Europe, Southern Europe, Mexico, Middle East

With a name that is French for "arm of honor," this gesture is known all over the world thanks to its on-field popularity with professional athletes. Signifying "Up yours," it is an outsize variation of the *doigt d'honneur* (or middle finger), whose grand scale makes it particularly well suited to arena sports. Be warned, however, that it remains illegal in some countries, such as Malta.

Despite its popularity among sportsmen, you need not be athletically inclined to use it yourself. Simply bend the arm at the elbow in an L-shape, using your other arm to grab on just below the bicep. If you wish to gild the lily, you may raise the middle finger of the bent arm.

"Up yours."

FIST THRUST

Meaning: Up yours.
Used in: Lebanon, Pakistan, Syria

Yet another way of signaling "Up yours," this particular incarnation suggests a circumference and degree of force that most would find quite uncomfortable. A regional variation of the Bras d'Honneur (page 116), it is guaranteed to cause great offense in parts of the Middle East.

"Up yours."

THUMBS-UP

Meaning: Up yours.
Used in: Greece, Latin America, Middle East, Russia, Sardinia, western Africa

Evolutionary biologists agree that the thumb originated millions of years ago. As for when the thumbs-up gesture originated, however, that remains unclear. Whatever its origins, its significance varies. Often, it just means approval. But in some countries, especially Latin American ones, it came to mean not "Sounds good" or "Could you give me a lift?" or "You should see this movie," but rather an invitation to insert the thumb intra-anally. Visitors to these regions should take care to keep their thumbs tucked well away unless offense is your intent. For extra insult, jerk upward.

NOTE: In Turkey, the gesture is often an invitation to homosexual relations.

"Up yours."

V

Meaning: Up yours.
Used in: United Kingdom, Australia, New Zealand

Known as the "two-fingered salute" or the "forks," this gesture is particular to the United Kingdom and its former colonies. Scholars believe that the gesture may have originated during the Norman invasion. When English archers were captured, it's said the French would cut off their index and middle fingers. At the Battle of Agincourt, when the French were badly defeated, English archers taunted French soldiers by flashing their intact fingers, and thus, perhaps, the V gesture was born.

The V differs from the peace sign in that the palm faces in. The two should not be confused, as good vibes will not result.

"Up yours."

FIG

Meaning: Up yours. Screw you. Would you like me to screw you?
Used in: Belgium, Denmark, France, Germany, Greece, Holland, India, Italy, Korea, Tunisia, Turkey

Known as the *fica* (or "fig") this gesture was common in ancient Rome, where it represented the reproductive sweetmeats, perhaps in the act of love. Over time it traveled to other countries; in some of which it was believed to have magical powers that could break spells and ward off evil.

The Fig remains a commonly used gesture throughout Europe and parts east, though its meaning varies from region to region. In some, it retains its original sexual connotation; in others, it is a good luck gesture meant to dispel bad fortune; and in still others, it is a profane insult. To execute, simply make a fist with the thumb protruding between the index and middle finger. Given the Fig's widely varying meanings, the savvy traveler will avoid playing "got your nose" with his host's children, lest an extremely awkward reaction result.

NOTE: In Japan, this is the sign for *sekkusu* (or "sex"). Its use in Japan is believed to date back to the Edo period (1603–1868), but it is rarely seen today.

"Screw you."

125

OK

Meaning: Orifice

Used in: Brazil, Germany, Greece, Italy, Malta, Mexico, Middle East, Paraguay, Russia, Tunisia, Turkey

"OK" is a near-universal word. The OK gesture, however, does not translate as easily. For as the inexperienced traveler quickly learns, in many countries, it is not a gesture of approval, but a graphic representation of a delicate orifice. The orifice in question varies regionally—sometimes male and sometimes female, sometimes ventral and sometimes dorsal. The intent, however, is always crude and usually insulting.

"Stick it in your orifice."